T0108988

Gap Analysis and Alternatives Analysis of the Coast Guard Cost Estimating Workforce

IRV BLICKSTEIN, TIM CONLEY, BRYNN TANNEHILL,
ABBY SCHENDT, JASON MICHEL ETCHEGARAY

PREPARED FOR THE U.S. COAST GUARD

Published in 2018

Preface

This report briefly summarizes a gap analysis and an alternatives analysis of the Coast Guard cost-estimating workforce. Researchers reviewed required cost-analysis documentation from Congress, the Government Accountability Office, the Department of Homeland Security (DHS), and the Coast Guard itself. In addition, this research draws on interviews with an extensive portion of the Coast Guard acquisition staff. This research should interest the broader Coast Guard acquisition and financial communities as well as the DHS Cost Analysis Division.

This research was sponsored by the U.S. Coast Guard and conducted within the Strategy, Policy, and Operations Program of the Homeland Security Operational Analysis Center (HSOAC), a federally funded research and development center (FFRDC) operated by the RAND Corporation under contract with DHS.

About the Homeland Security Operational Analysis Center

The Homeland Security Act of 2002 (Section 305 of PL 107-296, as codified in 6 U.S.C. 185), herein referred to as the "Act," authorizes the Secretary of DHS, acting through the Under Secretary for Science and Technology, to establish one or more FFRDCs to provide independent analysis of homeland security issues. The RAND Corporation operates HSOAC as an FFRDC for DHS under contract HSHQDC-16-D-00007.

The HSOAC FFRDC provides the U.S. government with independent and objective analyses and advice in core areas important to DHS in support of policy development, decisionmaking, alternative approaches, and new ideas on issues of significance. The HSOAC FFRDC also works with and supports other federal, state, local, tribal, and public- and private-sector organizations that make up the homeland security enterprise. The HSOAC FFRDC's research is undertaken by mutual consent with DHS and is organized as a set of discrete tasks. This report presents the results of research and analysis conducted under contract HSCG23-17-J-ADW016, titled "Gap Analysis and Alternatives Analysis of the Coast Guard Cost Estimating Workforce."

The results presented in this report do not necessarily reflect official DHS opinion or policy.

For more information on the Homeland Security Operational Analysis Center, see www.rand.org/hsoac.

For more information on this publication, visit www.rand.org/t/RR2047.

Contents

Figures and Tables

Figures

Tables

Summary

Background and Purpose

Uniformed services need to buy a wide range of equipment, including such major items as ships and aircraft. The U.S. Coast Guard currently is acquiring such major items in the form of new surface ships, including the national security cutter, the offshore patrol cutter, and the polar icebreaker. The Coast Guard wants to procure this equipment as cost effectively as possible, and pressure to bring these programs in on cost and schedule has grown with the new administration. In addition, Congress, the Department of Homeland Security (DHS), and the Coast Guard itself all have requirements pertaining to the acquisition process. To meet all these needs, an effective cost-estimating capability is critical to inform leadership decisions. However, unlike the other military services, the Coast Guard does not have its own capability to estimate procurement and life-cycle costs; it typically relies on other organizations to estimate the costs of acquiring its systems.

From the Coast Guard's perspective, relying on outside assistance for cost analysis creates several problems. First, the Coast Guard lacks visibility into the cost-calculating methods and assumptions of the proprietary models that private-sector contractors use to estimate costs. Second, different Coast Guard programs use different cost-estimating models for each equipment system. As a result, it can be difficult to maintain consistency across estimates. Third, the Coast Guard does not have the capability to conduct subsequent "what-if" analyses because the organizations that did the original analyses may no longer be under contract, and the Coast Guard may no longer have the necessary information. These challenges suggest that the Coast Guard needs more cost-estimating capability to assess affordability issues.

This Homeland Security Operational Analysis Center (HSOAC) report assesses the capabilities of the current Coast Guard cost-estimating workforce; identifies current requirements and current and future demands for cost-estimating services, based on Coast Guard acquisition plans; and recommends staffing and organizational alternatives to achieve flexibility to deal with future requirements.

Gaps in the Current Process

We were asked to independently assess the gaps in Coast Guard cost-estimating workforce and examine ways to improve the efficiency and effectiveness of the cost-estimating capability. Through an extensive interview process, we identified a number of gaps in the cost-estimating process. First, it is difficult to make cross-program comparisons of life-cycle costs. Program managers (PMs) are responsible for only their own program's life-cycle cost estimate (LCCE), so there is no incentive to use a consistent structure and methodology across the Coast Guard.

Each program can use different data sets and generate uniquely formatted reports. Second, questions from Coast Guard leaders often have follow-up questions after the initial cost estimate, and it is difficult to provide answers without in-house, in-depth knowledge of methods and models. Next, DHS requires an annual update of program LCCEs, but the Coast Guard does not collect and archive cost data. Finally, this lack of data makes it difficult to develop consistent and authoritative estimates for future systems.

Current Cost-Estimating Capabilities

Two organizations conduct most of the Coast Guard's cost analyses. Coast Guard (CG)–9283 is part of the Coast Guard's financial management directorate and conducts independent cost analyses for major acquisition programs. CG-93 is the Coast Guard's acquisition directorate, where cost analysts work for PMs to prepare LCCEs. Prior to acquisition decisions, these two cost analyses must be reconciled and approved by CG-928.

Based on data used in this analysis, the Coast Guard currently funds about 22 full-time equivalents (FTEs) to conduct cost analyses. CG-9283 has two full-time cost-estimating staff; neither has been certified to the Level III DHS Cost Estimating Standards, although one only lacks the years of experience to attain the Level III certification. The current ten major acquisition programs have approximately 20 FTEs from various external sources.

Alternatives to Fill Cost-Estimation Gaps

We assess that the Coast Guard has three alternatives to begin to mitigate these gaps. Each alternative has its advantages and disadvantages.

Alternative A: Continue CG-9283 and CG-93 as Separate Cost Activities

Alternative A maintains the status quo: CG-9283 keeps preparing totally independent cost estimates for major acquisition programs. This alternative would allow the CG-9283 staff to focus on unique issues within each cost analysis. It also would minimize the review cycle. However, if CG-9283 were tasked to perform the annual updates for major acquisition programs, it would require additional full-time billets, depending upon programmers' schedules.

However, of the three alternatives, Alternative A would be the least responsive to changes suggested by Congress, the Government Accountability Office, DHS, and Coast Guard documented leadership, as well as Coast Guard acquisition management's own requests for changes. CG-9283's small staff may make it difficult to deal with fluctuations in the workload and with each independent cost analysis. In addition, because of the opaque nature of cost estimation done by outside agencies, learning would not proliferate across the Coast Guard, and CG-9283 might not be able to interpret DHS cost methodologies.

Alternative B: Consolidate CG-9283 and CG-93 into Cost Competency Alignment

Creating a civilian-military competency-aligned division would align best with the changes recommended by both outside agencies and Coast Guard leadership. One supervisor would ensure a professional cost organization, and this supervisor and PMs can ensure that cost analysts achieve expected goals. This division would provide more flexibility to support changing requirements. It would also provide a single point of contact for leadership inquiries and a single communication channel between the Coast Guard and the Naval Sea System Command, the cost-analysis organization that performs or supports many of CG-93's current program cost estimates. Opportunities for career advancement would improve, and the need for short-term contract support would diminish. Finally, it would be possible to consolidate lessons learned and standardize cost data sources and methodologies.

The drawbacks to Alternative B include adding steps (and therefore time) to the cost-analysis review cycle. Program teams may be required to accept standard cost processes, and PMs would have less control over cost-estimating methodologies. It would also require greater cooperation between CG-9283 and CG-93. Finally, it might not be possible to get additional billets because of hiring freezes and efforts to reduce government personnel.

Alternative C: Use Contractor Support as Needed Within a Single Cost Division

Alternative C moderates between Alternatives A and B. Alternative C would retain a single cost division but would use a more varied mix of employee sources to develop the required cost products. This division should eventually progress to a primarily civil-service cost organization but may be able to strike a balance between civil-service employees, interservice agreements, and commercial contractors. The cost division would maintain centralized contracting authority to provide cost-analysis support to programs in CG-93 and CG-9283 and would ensure that all cost-analysis products meet the requirements of the Coast Guard and DHS processes.

Alternative C would need fewer direct hires and enable integration of government employees. It might also provide access to externally available proprietary data sources. It would enable the Coast Guard to focus cost expertise on a narrowly defined task.

Alternative C's drawbacks are that it would impede in-house learning, potentially cost more due to contracting, and require a contracting action. It would be more difficult to hold contract support to cost-division standards, and developing annual reports may be more difficult with less-stable contracting support. Also, the Coast Guard might not have full access to contractor methodologies, and contractors might not have access to government proprietary data.

Abbreviations

ACAT	Acquisition Category
ADA	Acquisition Decision Authority
ADE	Acquisition Decision Event
BCF	Business, Cost Estimating, and Financial Management
CAD	Cost Analyses Division of Homeland Security
CFO	chief financial officer
CG	Coast Guard (used for directorate designations)
CLB	Continuous Learning Business
DAU	Defense Acquisition University
DHS	Department of Homeland Security
EVM	earned-value management
FTE	full-time equivalent
FY	fiscal year
GAO	Government Accountability Office
HR	House Resolution
HSOAC	Homeland Security Operational Analysis Center
ICE	independent cost estimate
KSA	knowledge, skills, and abilities
LCCE	life-cycle cost estimate
MAOL	Master Acquisition Oversight List
NAVAIR	Naval Air Systems Command
NAVSEA	Naval Sea Systems Command
NCCA	Navy Center for Cost Analysis
PEO	program executive officer
PLCCE	program life-cycle cost estimate
PM	program manager

ROM	rough order of magnitude
SPAWAR	Space and Naval Warfare Systems Command
SYSCOM	systems command
TAC	total acquisition cost
TSA	Transportation Security Administration
WBS	work breakdown structure

1. Introduction

Background and Purpose

While the U.S. Coast Guard does not buy as many major items of equipment as the other military services, it still must acquire various items of equipment to carry out its mission. These include large and complex ships and aircraft, such as fast-response cutters, icebreakers, and long-range surveillance aircraft. Cost-effective acquisition requires good cost estimation to inform leadership decisions and facilitate trade-offs. However, the Coast Guard does not have the in-house cost-estimating capability to meet current Coast Guard and Department of Homeland Security (DHS) requirements. Instead, it turns to other organizations, usually the Naval Air Systems Command (NAVAIR) for aircraft and the Naval Sea Systems Command (NAVSEA) for ships, to prepare acceptable cost estimates.

This approach is fraught with problems. Coast Guard contracting for cost-estimation services can involve lengthy negotiations, preventing timely decisionmaking. In addition, because multiple organizations estimate costs for the Coast Guard, cost-estimating procedures are not properly standardized. Finally, Coast Guard personnel are unfamiliar with cost-estimating processes and cannot access models' data and methods. Therefore, Coast Guard personnel cannot always fully understand how estimates are derived.

The Homeland Security Operational Analysis Center (HSOAC) was asked to assess the capabilities of the current cost-estimating workforce; identify current requirements and current and future demands for cost-estimating services based on the Coast Guard *Major Systems Acquisition Manual*;[1] and develop staffing organizational alternatives to achieve a robust capability for future requirements. We were tasked to include a report on alternatives with recommendations to improve the Coast Guard cost-estimating workforce, including the following considerations:

1. change in the number of cost analysts
2. change in the source of cost analysts (government or contractor)
3. change in workforce organizational structure, including an assessment of centralized or distributed cost-estimating capabilities.

Research Approach

Our research began with a review of current guidance and recommendations from Congress, the Government Accountability Office (GAO), and DHS to the Coast Guard related to reporting

---

[1] U.S. Coast Guard, Acquisition Directorate, *Major Systems Acquisition Manual (MSAM)*, Commandant Instruction M5000.10D, May 29, 2015.

1

requirements for major acquisition programs and, more specifically, recommendations related to cost analysis. We also reviewed U.S. Navy cost-analysis activities for Naval Center for Cost Analysis (NCCA), NAVSEA, NAVAIR, and Space and Naval Warfare Systems Command (SPAWAR).

To understand Coast Guard directives and guidance for cost analysis, we reviewed instructions and plans, including the following:

- U.S. Coast Guard, *Coast Guard Acquisition Management Roles and Responsibilities*, Commandant Instruction 5000.12, July 6, 2012.
- U.S. Coast Guard, *Reimbursable Standard Rates*, Commandant Instruction 7310.1Q, October 16, 2015.
- U.S. Coast Guard, *Acquisition Directorate Strategic Plan: Blueprint for Sustained Excellence*, version 6.1, Summer 2016.
- U.S. Coast Guard, Acquisition Directorate, *Major Systems Acquisition Manual (MSAM)*, Commandant Instruction M5000.10D, May 29, 2015.
- U.S. Coast Guard, Acquisition Directorate, *Non-Major Acquisition Process (NMAP) Manual*, Commandant Instruction M5000.11B, December 2012.
- U.S. Department of Homeland Security, "Acquisition Management Directive," Directive Number: 102-01, Revision Number 3, July 28, 2015.
- U.S. Department of Homeland Security, *United States Coast Guard, Fiscal Year 2017: Congressional Justification*, 2016. (The Coast Guard has 13 projects/programs on the Master Acquisition Oversight List [MAOL].)

To develop an understanding of the current status Coast Guard cost-analysis organizational structure we conducted a series of interviews with Coast Guard and DHS organizations, as indicated in Table 1.1.

Table 1.1. Interviewed Organizations

Coast Guard Staff	Programs	External
CG-9; Acquisition Executive	Offshore patrol craft	DHS Cost Analysis Division
CG-924; Acquisition Support	Rescue 21	DHS Cost Analyst at the
CG-928; Resource Management	Polar icebreaker	Coast Guard
CG-821; Budget Development	In-service vessel sustainment	TSA Cost Organization
CG-6; Command, Control, Communications, and Computers and Information Technology		
CG-41; Aeronautical Engineering		
CG-45; Engineering and Logistics		

NOTE: "CG" followed by numbers indicates a Coast Guard directorate; TSA = Transportation Security Administration.

During the information gathering and subsequent analysis, we worked closely with Coast Guard leadership to understand Coast Guard cost-analysis requirements and analysts, supervisors, and decisionmakers' perceptions of the cost products delivered.

2. Congressional, Government Accountability Office, Department of Homeland Security, and Coast Guard Requirements

We reviewed congressional, GAO, DHS, and Coast Guard requirements for and guidance on cost analysis and estimation. Among other things, this review helped identify gaps in cost-analysis capabilities and possible alternatives to correct deficiencies noted by the several organizations.

Legislation That May Affect Cost Estimation

Three pieces of pending legislation may affect cost estimating at the Coast Guard. House Resolution (HR) 347, if passed into law, would require the head of a component office to maintain accurate and up-to-date documentation with a complete life-cycle cost estimate (LCCE) and verification of the LCCE through an independent cost estimate (ICE).[2] It would also require the preparation of cost estimates for major programs in a manner consistent with GAO standards and submission of acquisition documents to DHS for an annual comprehensive report on status of acquisitions. The resolution contains a few exceptions to the requirements outlined.

HR 1252 intends to expand the authority and/or responsibility of the Under Secretary of Management of DHS. It establishes the Office of Program Accountability and Risk Management to provide oversight and consistent accountability, standardization, and transparency for all major acquisitions.[3]

HR 1365 allows the Under Secretary of Management of DHS to assign an individual to manage acquisition innovation, test emerging acquisition management directives, develop best practices and lessons learned (for acquisitions throughout the department), and establish metrics for effectiveness. It also calls for more-stringent reporting requirements.[4]

GAO Requirements

Coast Guard acquisition has been the subject of three GAO assessments related to cost estimation. A 2017 assessment resulted in a DHS memorandum to the GAO about corrective

---

[2] U.S. House of Representatives, DHS Acquisition Documentation Integrity Act of 2017, 115th Cong., 1st sess., H.R. 347, January 31, 2017a.

[3] U.S. House of Representatives, DHS Acquisition Authorities Act of 2017, 115th Cong., 1st sess., H.R. 1252, March 21, 2017b.

[4] U.S. House of Representatives, "Department of Homeland Security Acquisition Innovation Act," 115th Cong., 1st sess., H.R. 1365, March 27, 2017c.

action taken in response. The second GAO assessment dealt with oversight and congressional reporting. A 2015 GAO assessment pertained to cost-estimating guides.

A 2017 GAO assessment of the Coast Guard cost estimates for the fast response cutter and national security cutter found that

> the Coast Guard did not document its cost analyses, in accordance with GAO cost estimating best practices. Without such documentation, the Coast Guard cannot demonstrate that it is making cost-effective decisions.[5]

In response, DHS assured that the

> Coast Guard Assistant Commandant for Acquisition (CG-9) and Assistant Commandant for Engineering and Logistics (CG-4) communities will collaborate to determine a consistent, repeatable cost benefit analysis methodology to be considered with other factors.[6]

In March 2015, the GAO released a report about the requirements and practices of DHS's acquisition guidelines.[7] In the report, GAO outlined several key problems, including a lack of approval for sustainment costs, a lack of key cost information for programs, and a lack of performance and documentation of cost-estimate updates. GAO's emphasis on the importance of cost estimates would later be repeated in a January 2016 DHS memo, which stated that "accurate, credible, comprehensive and well-documented estimates are critical for making proactive resource allocation decisions and providing early warning of issues."[8]

GAO's 2015 report listed the requirements for the annual Comprehensive Acquisition Status Report. Some of the key requirements were

1. cost risk analysis
2. earned-value management (EVM) data
3. procurement schedule and annual cost estimates
4. reasons for significant change from previous the Comprehensive Acquisition Status Report
5. comparisons of the current baseline estimate and the original.[9]

While this list is not exhaustive, these are significant features that require dedicated personnel to monitor the cost of a project as it moves from the analyze and select phase to the end of its sustainment phase. The January 2016 DHS memo added the requirement that a work

---

[5] GAO, "Coast Guard Cutters: Depot Maintenance Is Affecting Operational Availability and Cost Estimates Should Reflect Actual Expenditures," Report to the Chairman, Subcommittee on Coast Guard and Maritime Transportation, Committee on Transportation and Infrastructure, House of Representatives, March 2017.

[6] Jim H. Crumpacker, "DHS Management Response to Recommendations Contained in GAO-17-218," Department of Homeland Security, February 16, 2017.

[7] GAO, *Homeland Security Acquisitions: DHS Should Better Define Oversight Roles and Improve Program Reporting to Congress*, GAO-15-292, March 2015.

[8] DHS, "Memo for Annual Cost Estimates," January 11, 2016.

[9] GAO, 2015.

breakdown structure (WBS) would also be tracked in the annual update comparing the prior WBS and the current WBS.

The *GAO Cost Estimating and Assessment Guide* contains recommendations for best practices.[10] It presents case studies, the basic framework for cost estimates (see Figure 2.1), and detailed descriptions of how to perform each cost-estimating function. It also lays out the 12-step cost-estimating process, which is also part of the DHS and Coast Guard cost-estimation guidance.[11]

Figure 2.1. GAO Recommended Cost-Estimating Process

Initiation and research	Assessment	Analysis	Presentation
Your audience, what you are estimating, and why you are estimating it are of the utmost importance	Cost assessment steps are iterative and can be accomplished in varying order or concurrently	The confidence in the point or range of the estimate is crucial to the decision maker	Documentation and presentation make or break a cost estimating decision outcome

Analysis, presentation, and updating the estimate steps can lead to repeating previous assessment steps

Define the estimate's purpose → Develop the estimating plan → [Define the program / Obtain the data] → [Determine the estimating structure / Develop the point estimate and compare it to an independent cost estimate] → [Identify ground rules and assumptions] → Conduct sensitivity → Conduct a risk and uncertainty analysis → Document the estimate → Present estimate to management for approval → Update the estimate to reflect actual costs/changes

SOURCE: GAO, 2009.

The GAO guide strongly encourages the development and use of an EVM system. The framework recommended for the EVM is based on Program Management Institute standards. The purpose of an EVM system is to provide a way to measure actual performance against an approved baseline plan. The EVM relies on an accurate timeline and WBS. It is worth noting that the Coast Guard does not have an EVM system in place, according to interviews.

DHS Cost-Estimate Requirements

DHS requirements or guidance of cost estimating appear in formal instructions, in department briefing templates, and in DHS requirements for an analysis of alternatives.

DHS Acquisition Management Instruction 102-01-001

DHS Acquisition Management Instruction 102-01-001 (2016) differs from the 2009 DHS Acquisition Management Instruction in that it delineates responsibilities of senior DHS

---

[10] GAO, *GAO Cost Estimating and Assessment Guide: Best Practices for Developing and Managing Capital Programs and Costs*, Washington, D.C, GAO-09-3SP, March 2009.

[11] GAO, 2009.

leadership in acquisition programs, including LCCE development. It focuses on the roles, authority, and responsibilities of positions, such as chief financial officers (CFOs), and less on methodology and program-level details.

The DHS Acquisition Management Instruction states that an LCCE provides

> an exhaustive and structured accounting of all past (or sunk), present, and future resources and associated cost elements required to develop, produce, deploy, sustain and dispose of a particular system (program) regardless of funding sources.[12]

The DHS CFO has the authority to approve major acquisition program LCCEs and develop ICEs (determining a cost) and independent cost analyses (justifying that cost) to be used as tools in acquisition decisions. The component acquisition executive has oversight requirements that include approving cost-estimating baseline documents for any Undersecretary for Management–directed ICEs developed by the CFO.

The original designation of the program level is made using the rough-order-of-magnitude (ROM) estimate from the component acquisition executive with input from the executive director, program accountability and risk management officer, and the CFO. The LCCE should be developed during the alternatives analysis phase to support the preferred solution. Any acquisition program baseline revisions (including performance, cost, and schedule changes) require an approved LCCE, unless the Cost Analysis Division (CAD) CFO determined that the latest cost estimate remains valid. The management instruction requires the component senior financial officer and component acquisition executive to review and sign the LCCE and the office of the CFO to provide final approval. The cost-estimating baseline documents, if required, only require final approval from the component acquisition executive.

DHS Annual LCCE Update Briefing Template (2016)

While the DHS Annual LCCE Update Briefing template is not a regulation, it does show what is expected in practice. This briefing includes an annual update on the WBS, stating which fiscal years (FYs) in the WBS are based on actual numbers; changes to the schedule; how the current LCCE update compares with the previous one; and a comparison of the updated LCCE to the acquisition program baseline.[13]

Analysis-of-Alternatives Methodologies: Considerations for DHS Acquisition Analysis (2014)

DHS's report on performing an analysis of alternatives states that "The analysis does not make the decision, but it informs the [analysis of alternatives] selection of a preferred

---

[12] U.S. Department of Homeland Security, "Acquisition Management Instruction," DHS Instruction 102-01-001, Revision 1, March 19, 2016.

[13] Tracy Tenwalde, "DHS Annual LCCE Update Briefing Template," U.S. Coast Guard CG-0283, January 16, 2017.

alternative."[14] The analysis of alternatives report does include a ROM cost estimate and analysis, but the program manager (PM) must submit several other "cost-related documents" to prepare the first program LCCE (PLCCE). Some of the documents that should be submitted for each program in consideration are the following:

1. acquisition plan
2. acquisition program baseline
3. cost-estimating baseline document
4. WBS
5. sensitivity analysis on cost and effectiveness measures.

During the analysis of alternatives, DHS considers the cost-estimating guidance to require only a ROM estimate and may not require dedicated support from a cost analyst.

Coast Guard Cost-Estimate Requirements

The Coast Guard has its own documents pertaining to cost estimating, including its *Major Systems Acquisition Manual.*[15] We derived the requirements for Coast Guard cost estimation from Chapters 1, 2, and 5 of this manual.

The Coast Guard's major systems acquisition life cycle is shown in Figure 2.2.

Figure 2.2. Coast Guard Major Systems Acquisition Life-Cycle Framework

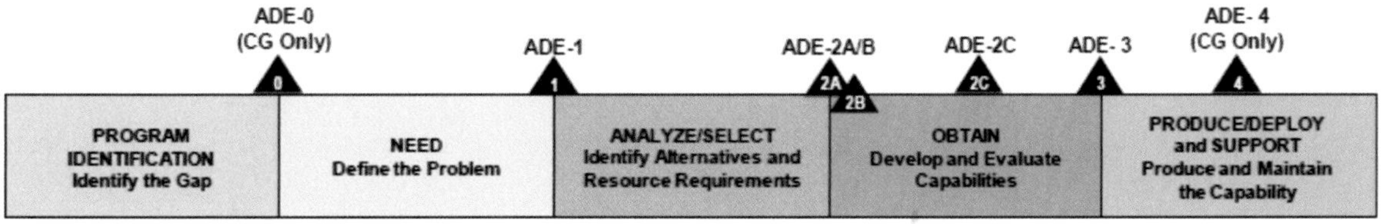

SOURCE: U.S. Coast Guard, 2015.

The initial cost estimate for any prospective program occurs during the Program Identification Phase acquisition decision event (ADE-0). During this phase, ROM cost estimates are used to gauge the potential cost of a proposed new program. These estimates inform decisionmakers of what material solutions may be feasible and supports development of a capital investment plan. The material solutions suggested by the ROM and the capital investment plan feed into the alternatives analysis.

The PM is responsible for developing high-fidelity cost estimates for major acquisitions. Promising concepts are evaluated using an alternatives analysis, including costs based on a ROM cost estimate. The alternatives analysis

---

[14] Bryant Streett et al., *Analysis of Alternatives (AoA) Methodologies: Considerations for DHS Acquisition Analysis*, Falls Church, Va.: Homeland Security Studies and Analysis Institute, January 22, 2014.

[15] U.S. Coast Guard, 2015.

shall be conducted by an independent third party such as a federally funded research and development center, a qualified entity of the DOD, or similar independent organization that has appropriate acquisition experience.[16]

The sponsor will work with the third party to compare operational requirements with the cost estimates and adjust accordingly.

After the needs phase, cost-estimating baseline documents are developed for the preferred alternative. The cost-estimating baseline documents define the programmatic and technical characteristics for the LCCE and the ICE. The ICE is effectively an independently developed LCCE. Nonmajor programs do not require an ICE. LCCE development should be led by a Level III DHS Cost Estimating Standards–qualified business cost estimator or equivalent. The Coast Guard recommends using the 12 steps listed in the *GAO Cost Estimating and Assessment Guide* as a framework to develop the LCCE.[17]

An ICE will be developed for every major acquisition program in support of the ADE-2 decision. *Independent* means "the preparation of the estimate by an office or entity that is not under the supervision, direction, advocacy, or control of the PEO [program executive officer] or Sponsor." The ICE will be based on a common set of government-furnished assumptions, but the methods used are up to the independent agent. One of the common inputs between the LCCE and the ICE is the WBS. If a contractor develops the ICE, the PM "should include a requirement for the contractor to deliver an editable electronic cost model to support future updates to the LCCE."[18]

Acquisitions are classified according to the LCCE and total acquisition cost (TAC). These classifications determine the level of oversight by the Under Secretary for Management as the acquisition decision authority (ADA) and are divided into levels 1 and 2 (major) and level 3 (nonmajor), as detailed in Table 2.1. The Coast Guard currently has 13 major and 11 nonmajor programs.

---

[16] Coast Guard, 2015.

[17] GAO, 2009.

[18] Coast Guard, 2015.

Table 2.1. Determining Acquisition Level

Acquisition Level	Qualifications for Level
Level 1 (Major)	LCCE equals or exceeds $1 billion or TAC exceeds $300 million ADA: Under Secretary for Management
Level 2 (Major)	LCCE equals or exceeds $300 million, but less than $1 billion or TAC exceeds $100 million but less than $300 million ADA: Under Secretary for Management designated or component acquisition executive
Level 3 (Minor)	LCCE less than $100 million ADA: see Table 3

SOURCE: U.S. Coast Guard, 2015.

Once the LCCE and the ICE have been developed, they are reconciled by the PM and CG-928 to produce the PLCCE. Estimates that cannot be reconciled at this level will be briefed to CG-9 and reconciled at that level.

The PLCCE must be certified by the DHS CAD and is required to support the ADE-2A/B, ADE-2C, and ADE-3 milestone decisions. The PLCCE must be maintained and updated any time a major program changes, acquisition program baseline revisions occur, or ADE-2 through -3 decisions are made. Subsequent, similar updates to the ICE are not required. PMs will also review PLCCEs annually to determine whether significant changes in cost have occurred or are likely to occur.

Nonmajor acquisitions are governed by the Coast Guard's *Non-Major Acquisition Process (NMAP) Manual*.[19] CG-9 is the chair for nonmajor, non–information technology programs, and CG-6 is the chair for nonmajor information technology programs.

Coast Guard Not Meeting All Requirements

Current LCCE Process Gaps

Methodologies can vary across programs and make cross-program comparisons difficult. Since PMs are responsible for only their own LCCEs, each program can use different data sets and generate uniquely formatted reports. This can benefit individual programs, but it makes comparing analyses from different programs difficult. Conducting an ICE requires CG-9283 analysts to work with each program cost team and understand the unique elements of each program estimate. Since there are only two full-time analysts, they rely even more heavily on the expertise of contracted cost-analysis support, including from other government agencies.

---

[19] U.S. Coast Guard, Acquisition Directorate, *Non-Major Acquisition Process (NMAP) Manual*, Commandant Instruction M5000.11B, December 2012.

Unfulfilled DHS Requirements

Unfulfilled requirements create a number of gaps as well. Currently, a senior cost analyst is assigned from DHS headquarters to help programs prepare LCCEs for DHS approval. When this analyst's assignment is complete, there will still be a full-time requirement to conduct quality assurance of cost estimates to ensure they meet Coast Guard and DHS requirements. During an interview with officials from TSA, they acknowledged that the assistance from DHS was extremely helpful.[20] They also noted that they had to take on the additional work of verifying that cost estimates were submitted in accordance with DHS guidance when the DHS analyst was reassigned.

A second gap is the provision of annual updates to PLCCEs. This additional tasking is over and above the original intent of the *Major Systems Acquisition Manual*.[21] The Coast Guard has indicated that it has neither the data nor the resources to provide these annual updates, but DHS has indicated that the requirement will not be relaxed. In addition, CG-82 (the Coast Guard's budgeting activity) reported that its accounting system can be realigned to meet the annual reporting requirement, but this functionality will not be available until after 2020.

A third gap is that the Coast Guard is not collecting and archiving executed cost data in a format that can be used for analogous data in future systems. The new cost accounting system does not currently have a requirement to provide execution cost data in a format suitable for cost analysis. Maintenance data for ships and aircraft are collected and available to track historical system performance, but these two logistic information systems are not tailored to support cost analysis. NAVSEA and other Department of Defense cost estimators are assumed to have sufficient credentials to perform cost analysis, but the Coast Guard has used commercial contractors who turned out to be unqualified to complete a life-cycle cost analysis. This resulted in CG-9283 having to take over the cost analysis and prepare suitable LCCEs.

As of the beginning of 2017, the CG-9283 cost-analysis organization consisted of two full-time analysts, neither of whom had Level III certifications as cost analysts. However, the civilian cost estimator, hired in December 2016, has Level II certification and is nearing completion of the requirements to obtain a Level III certification (certification requirements for cost analysts are described in Chapter 5). CG-93 major program cost estimates have been the responsibility of the PM and typically provided by contractors or interservice agreements with NAVSEA.

---

[20] Interview with TSA staff, March 1, 2017.

[21] U.S. Coast Guard, 2015.

3. Coast Guard Cost-Analysis Capabilities Compared with U.S. Navy

As we will show later, the Coast Guard's acquisition budget is smaller than that of the U.S. Navy. It is, however, helpful to understand how the U.S. Navy treats cost analysis, the size of its organizations, the functional diversity of the cost organizations, and the types of functions these cost organizations perform. This chapter is a brief description of that capability and diversity.

The Coast Guard has received assistance from the U.S. Navy for cost analyses for many years and has developed the following relationships:

1. **NAVSEA cost organization, SEA 05C, for ships.** 05C personnel perform the cost analysis directly if workload permits or contract analysis to commercial companies involved in the cost estimation of ships.
2. **NAVAIR cost-analysis organization, AIR 4.2, for aircraft.** AIR 4.2 provides either direct or contracted and supervised services to the Coast Guard.
3. **SPAWAR for command, control, communications, and intelligence systems.**
4. **NCCA for ICEs.** Some program offices indicated that they used this organization.

NAVSEA, NAVAIR, and SPAWAR consider cost analysis to be a command core competency, equal to engineering, contracting, and financial management. All three commands have organizations dedicated to performing estimates for acquisition, procurement, and life-cycle costs for supported PEOs and PMs. No organization within the Coast Guard considers cost analysis to be a core competency in support of PEOs and PMs. Please note that not all cost organizations in the Navy perform the same functions. In some cases, they perform mainly cost analysis for systems under procurement. In others, that analysis expands to life-cycle cost analyses, schedule analyses, earned-value analyses, and facilities analyses. Each is unique to the management structure of the command and its relationship to the PEO structure in that command.

NCCA is somewhat unique because its responsibilities include serving as the principal adviser to Department of the Navy leadership on issues of cost; developing ICEs for Acquisition Category (ACAT) IC, ACAT IAC, and ACAT IAM programs; [22] independently assessing system command (SYSCOM)–generated program LCEEs for all ACAT I programs (and for ACAT II

---

[22] ACAT I programs are Major Defense Acquisition programs. *IC* refers to programs for which the Department of Defense component head is the decisionmaking authority. ACAT IA programs are Major Automated Information Systems acquisition programs. *IAC* refers to programs for which the Department of Defense Chief Information Officer has delegated authority to the head of the component. *IAM* refers to programs for which the Under Secretary of Defense for Acquisition, Technology and Logistics is the decisionmaking authority.

programs, as directed by the Assistant Secretary of the Navy, Financial Management and Comptroller); and chairing the Department of the Navy cost review boards.[23]

Staffing of the functions in the Department of the Navy is shown in Table 3.1. In comparison, the TSA has six cost estimators conducting ICEs and performing annual LCCE updates. The number and complexity of estimators preparing individual PLCCEs for TSA procurement is far less than either the Coast Guard or the Navy, and we present Coast Guard numbers later in this report.

Table 3.1. Department of the Navy Cost-Estimating in Full-Time Equivalents, Plus TSA

Command	Total	Contractors	Government Employees
SPAWAR	69	26	43
SEA 05C	113	7	106
NAVAIR	417	38	379
U.S. Marine Corps	71	18	52
NCCA	71	16	54
TSA	6	Unknown	6

The range of functions that the cost-estimating community in the Navy performs varies:

- SYSCOM reporting of cost and analysis personnel varies significantly depending on SYSCOM-specific implementation of cost-estimating tasks. For example, NAVAIR 4.2 defines schedule analysis, scheduling operations and support, integrated product support (beyond LCCEs), budget support, and broader analytical and cost support as significant cost-estimating tasks. Cost-estimating personnel working on EVM tasks range from four in Marine Corps Systems Command to 62 in NAVAIR (over 75 percent of personnel are at NAVAIR).
- In NAVSEA, this issue is complicated by NAVSEA 05C having limited visibility into cost-estimating personnel for lower ACAT programs. PEOs and PMs, not SEA 05C, contract for EVM activities.
- Additionally, oversight of cost personnel varies among SYSCOMs. NAVAIR 4.2 and Marine Corps Systems Command Cost and Analyses oversee all cost personnel for their SYSCOMs, but NAVSEA 05C has limited insight into cost estimates and cost personnel for lower ACAT and abbreviated acquisition programs, where cost personnel are directly hired by PEOs or PMs.

In recent years, ICEs were required for all major defense acquisition programs,[24] and the Secretary of the Navy required NCCA to accomplish the following:[25]

---

[23] Secretary of the Navy, Instruction 5223.2A, "Department of the Navy Cost Analysis," Washington, D.C.: Department of the Navy, December 3, 2012a.

[24] Department of Defense, "Operation of the Defense Acquisition System," Department of Defense Instruction 5000.02, January 7, 2012, revised February 2, 2017.

[25] Secretary of the Navy, 2012.

- Complete ICEs for all ACAT IC and IAC programs, for which the Department of the Navy is the milestone decision authority.
- Accomplish an independent cost assessment for all ACAT ID and IAM programs for which the Office of the Secretary of Defense is the milestone decision authority before the Office of the Secretary of Defense, Cost Analysis and Program Evaluation performs the ICE.

Comparing the organizations just listed can be fraught with difficulty, but Figure 3.1 compares these organizations, depicting cost-estimating workforces on the Y-axis and the procurement budgets managed by the organization on the X-axis. When only the two full-time equivalents (FTEs) in CG-9283 are considered, the Coast Guard clearly does not have enough personnel dedicated to cost analysis. As indicated on the chart by the point labeled "USCG," closer to 20 FTEs of effort are dedicated to cost analysis in CG-93.

Figure 3.1. Comparison of Cost-Analysis Billets (in Full-Time Equivalents) Versus Procurement Budget Authority

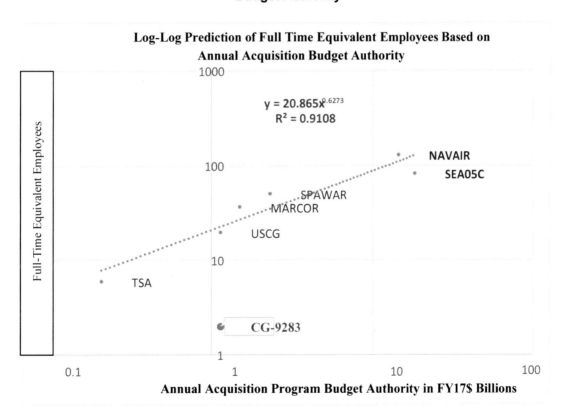

NOTE: MARCOR = U.S. Marine Corps; USCG = U.S. Coast Guard.

Figure 3.2 shows types of functions that cost analysts in the Department of the Navy perform and the relative amount of effort toward each function in 2014. Table 3.2 provides more details on the levels of effort associated with the various functions that these analysts perform and indicates the broad types of duties.

Figure 3.2. Percentage of Effort by Area

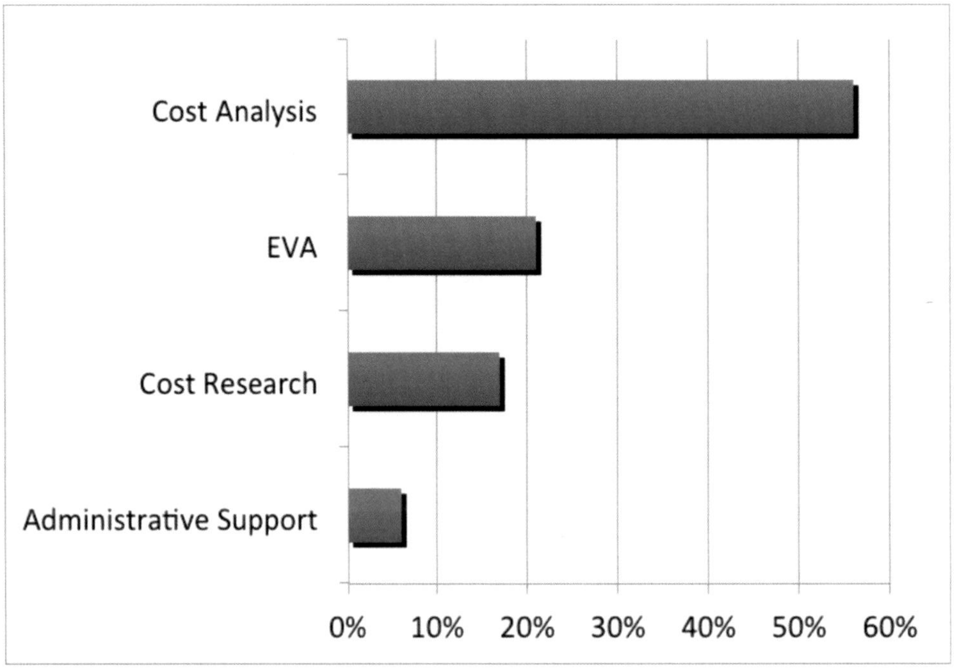

NOTE: EVA = earned-value analysis.

Table 3.2. Survey of Cost-Estimating Workforce Functions, Department of the Navy Working Group

Cost Estimating FTE On-board as of 30 Sep 2014

	Level I Functions	NCCA Gov't	NCCA Contractor	MCSC C&A Gov't	MCSC C&A Contractor	AIR 4.2 Gov't	AIR 4.2 Contractor	SEA 05C Gov't	SEA 05C Contractor	SPAWAR 1.6 Gov't	SPAWAR 1.6 Contractor	TOTAL Gov't	TOTAL Contractor
#1	Program Life Cycle Cost Estimating (PLCCE) (and supporting activities) for programs with OSD AT&L as MDA	0.3	0.1	3.8	0.2	8.0	1.0	36.4	3.5	9.8	7.2	58.3	12.0
#2	PLCCE (and supporting activities) for programs with DON (ASN RDA) as MDA			2.6		8.0	1.0	15.3	1.0	7.8	1.5	33.7	3.5
#3	PLCCE (and supporting activities) for programs with COMSYSCOM/PEO as MDA	2.3		3.8	2.1	5.0	1.0	9.0		8.5	7.7	28.6	10.8
#4	PLCCE (and supporting activities) for programs with PM as MDA			10.7	4.5	5.0		4.0		1.3	3.0	21.0	7.5
#5	PLCCE (and supporting activities) for other programs			0.3	2.0			4.9	1.7			5.2	3.7
#6	Service Cost Center (SCC) Life Cycle Cost Estimating (program specific) for programs with OSD AT&L as MDA	14.2	1.8									14.2	1.8
#7	SCC Life Cycle Cost Estimating (program specific) for programs with DON (ASN RDA) as MDA	8.6	0.9									8.6	0.9
#8	SCC Life Cycle Cost Estimating (program specific) for programs with COMSYSCOM/PEO as MDA												
#9	SCC Life Cycle Cost Estimating (program specific) for programs with PM as MDA												
#10	SCC Life Cycle Cost Estimating (program specific) for other programs	2.8	0.2									2.8	0.2
#11	Budget Support	0.9		0.8		58.0	8.0	3.3		1.6	0.8	64.5	8.8
#12	Contract Support	0.2		5.9		32.0	4.0	4.0		1.7		43.7	4.0
#13	Earned Value Management (EVM) Support	0.9	0.1	3.0	1.0	62.0	7.0	9.9		5.2		81.0	8.1
#14	Schedule Analysis and Scheduling	1.1		0.5	0.3	48.0	6.0	2.9				52.5	7.3
#15	Cost Research, Data, and Tools	11.7	12.0	2.2	3.5	17.0		3.2	0.3	2.4	1.0	36.5	15.8
#16	Cost Benefit Analysis	2.4	0.5	8.5	3.3	13.0	2.0	0.5		1.1	4.5	25.5	10.3
#17	O&S and IPS Support (Beyond LCCE Activities Above)	0.4	0.1	1.7		85.0		1.2				88.3	0.1
#18	Industrial Base Analyses					4.0		9.0				13.0	
#19	Broader Analytical/Cost Support	0.3		2.5	0.7	27.0	8.0			0.1		30.0	8.7
#20	Policy and Guidance	2.3				3.0		1.5		0.1		6.9	
#21	DON Cost Community/Personnel Support	5.3	0.3	6.9		14.0		1.0		3.5	0.3	30.6	0.3
	Non-DON Support	1.3										1.3	
	TOTAL	55.0	16.0	53.0	17.5	389.0	38.0	106.0	6.5	43.0	25.6	646.0	103.7
		71.0		70.5		427.0		112.5		68.6		749.6	

SOURCE: Center for Naval Analyses, "Evaluation of Systems Command Consolidation Options, Phase 2," July 2015.

15

4. Cost Analysis of Workload Demand

Defining the Coast Guard's cost-analysis workload depends on what is considered cost analysis. The *Major Systems Acquisition Manual* identifies a requirement that certified cost analysts conduct a PLCCE and a separate ICE for major acquisition programs.[26] PMs and integrated product teams include cost considerations as part of their analysis of alternatives and program design, before the formal LCCE. As acquisition programs progress and as leadership plans the support strategy, system engineers, logisticians, and budget analysts prepare initial cost estimates for operating expense budget planning. Cost analysts are not specifically required as part of the integrated product team structure until after the analysis of alternatives has determined the preferred solution.

In our interviews, there was almost unanimous agreement that cost estimating ought to be within the Coast Guard's internal capability. While the Navy has great expertise and was known to be very helpful, our interviews revealed the following issues:

- The models being used, particularly by the contractors, were proprietary; therefore, the Coast Guard was unable to certify the cost estimates. The issue arose as the estimates moved through the chain of command and, in particular, to DHS. Much like the Department of Defense's Cost Analysis and Program Evaluation office, the DHS CAD office is increasingly demanding that the models used by the Coast Guard and other DHS entities add transparency to their cost estimates.
- Management also wanted to be able to request modifications or changes to cost estimates as conditions or circumstances changed. During the budget process, "what if" questions arise about changes in quantity or the need to spread the procurement or maintenance action over longer periods. Those transactions require in-house personnel with the requisite knowledge of the models to respond to requests in a timely manner. We heard numerous comments about the time it takes to get a contractor on board and then deal with quality issues or the contractor's lack of understanding of Coast Guard in-house processes and data availability.
- There is also the issue of consistency. Each cost analysis uses a different contractor or government entity and uses them in a different way. Coast Guard management has difficultly relying on estimates developed outside the Coast Guard and from different organizations with differing motivations and loyalties.
- Finally, cost analyses can be used in the budget process to aid in the determination of affordability. While CG-82 appears self-sufficient, the Acquisition Directorate desires to play a greater role in determining the affordability of its systems and to use affordability considerations in the development and design of future ships, aircraft, and systems. Having a more robust in-house capability would help satisfy that desire.

---

[26] U.S. Coast Guard, 2015.

As a way to determine the acquisition program workload, we were provided a CG-93 cost-analysis budget exhibit for FY 2017, which was a mix of annual total dollars, hours, and (in some cases) specific job skills. The data identified five individuals for one program that were preparing documentation necessary to develop the LCCE, but not necessarily preparing the cost estimate. Initially, we excluded those FTEs and prepared our estimate for the number of cost analysts to specifically those who prepare the LCCE.

The data describing the number of FTEs in FY 2017 for CG-93 included total dollars per year for various tasks, without identifying the number of associated FTEs (see Figure 4.1). Other data specified the number of hours for tasks and identified the work that would require multiple individuals with different skills concurrently. Depending on how you estimate the value of a single FTE, the number of work hours that compose a full work year, and the number of different individuals that would be required for concurrent tasks, 12 to 15 people would be needed to conduct cost analysis from the data provided for six of the ten major programs in 2017.

As a cross check, the data also provided the FY 2017 total dollars budgeted for the six programs. Using FTE generic rates and depending on the mix of skill level and experience, the budget cost data support the estimate of 12 to 15 analysts.

After we estimated the number of cost analysts, we agreed that the five FTEs preparing cost-analysis documentation should be included and that the work to prepare cost-analysis documentation is inherently part of the LCCE process.

There is also a range in the number of FTEs necessary for CG-9283 to complete the current workload. We have described the two full-time cost analysts in CG-9283, but this organization typically includes additional contractor support for short-term projects. We have not included the cost or FTEs impact of this contract support. By analogy with annual cost-analysis updates conducted at NAVAIR, there will be a requirement for two additional cost analysts if CG-9283 is tasked to perform the annual major system LCCE updates.

Figure 4.1. FY 2017 CG-93 and CG-9283 Estimated Cost-Analysis Full-Time Equivalents

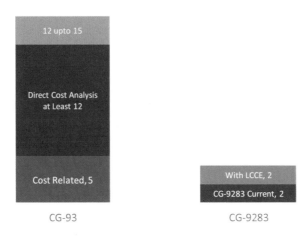

Table 4.1 provides the approximate number of funded FTEs for the ten programs on the Coast Guard FY 2017 MAOL, plus dedicated support for the 47-foot motor lifeboat, which was added to the MAOL in the July report. It was reported that the most current LCCEs for three programs were completed by CG-9283.

Table 4.1. FY 2017 Contract and/or Navy Support Full-Time Equivalents

CG-93 Program Contracted Cost-Estimating Support ($3.6 million)	Cost-Analyst Full-Time Equivalents (estimated)
Command, control, communications, computers, intelligence, surveillance and reconnaissance	1.4
Fast-response cutter	5.0
H-65 conversion-sustainment projects	0.7
Long-range surveillance aircraft (C-130H-J)	0.7
Medium-range surveillance aircraft	CG-9283 completed these estimates (1.4 work years). Contractor support was insufficient.
National-security cutter	
Nationwide Automatic Identification System	
Offshore patrol cutter	5.0
Polar icebreaker	6.0
Rescue 21	0.4
47-foot motor lifeboat[a]	0.5

NOTE: The FTE total does not include the one civilian and one military billet assigned to CG-9283.
[a] Not on the February 2017 MAOL.

These program estimates are subject to the Coast Guard *Major Systems Acquisition Manual* and the "scorecard review" by DHS CFO-CAD personnel.[27] The "scorecard" is based on the 12 essential elements of LCCEs described in the *GAO Cost Estimating and Assessment Guide*.

During interviews, Coast Guard officials identified cost-estimating activities conducted outside the formal life-cycle cost-analysis process. Throughout the operating years of a major ship or aircraft system, significant depot-level maintenance events require cost estimates to determine the amount of work that can be accomplished within budget constraints. Modifications to in-service systems also require separate cost estimates. Resource sponsors in CG-4 and CG-6 identified annual requirements to review cost data in their budget and long-range planning. Nonmajor programs do not have formal cost-analysis requirements, but leaders did comment that they devoted time and effort to determining the affordability of program decisions and the impact of budget shortfalls. No estimates were provided for the level of effort that might be required for these programs, but nonmajor program leaders would likely welcome in-house cost analysis.

U.S. government agencies take special care to account for how appropriated funds are spent. There are specific career certification requirements for contracting officers, financial managers,

---

[27] U.S. Coast Guard, 2015; GAO, 2009.

and cost analysts. The training for each career is unique, and a contracting officer or financial manager is not interchangeable with a cost analyst. Contracting officers and financial managers have unique obligations and are fiscally liable to accurately obligate funds and ensure that products and services are delivered. There are almost no situations where a PM or resources sponsor would choose to accept the burden of fiscal liability from the contracting officer or financial manager. This is not always the case for cost analysts.

Cost analysis will never achieve the level of accuracy needed to balance financial ledgers, but it does provide PMs and resource sponsors with estimates of how the government should execute millions of dollars. As resource decisions are made, LCCEs, analysis of alternatives, business case analyses, and other cost-analysis products form a baseline for future budgets and bargaining positions for contract negotiations.

Measuring the cost-analysis gap for the Coast Guard may in part be a determination of what portion of budgeting and forward projection of acquisition and sustainment requirements should be controlled in a thorough cost-analysis process and how much should remain with PMs, resource sponsors, and senior leadership. Our interviews with Coast Guard leaders found a wide range of recommendations. For organizations that choose to use cost analysis, the gap can be closed quickly. Others will continue to prepare cost products on their own, even though they might not avoid the use of other, similar financial career specialties. Determining how the cost-analysis gap will ultimately be filled depends almost completely on the value added.

During our interviews, CG-9283 and individuals in CG-93 indicated that there are consistently about ten major acquisition programs and that, about every three years, there is a new program that requires additional support to develop the initial PLCCE. Based on FY 2017 Coast Guard data, as described previously, we offer 12 to 15 FTEs as the cost-analysis requirement for Coast Guard planning purposes. An additional four or more work years are provided by NAVSEA technical expertise. Filling the gaps identified during our research will depend on efforts to optimize the use of the existing cost analysts to meet current program office requirements and accept some of the other "gapped" work. If cost analysts continue to be stovepiped to particular programs, any additional work will require additional funding. If cost analysts can be consolidated into a single organization to support program life-cycle cost estimating and separately support other cost-analysis projects, the Coast Guard may be able to increase the value of cost analysis within the current work force, while simultaneously achieving economies of scale and the benefits of centralized management for workload allocation. If a consolidated process is successful, incremental growth will depend on demand signals from PMs, resource sponsors, and Coast Guard leadership.

Acquisition program cost analyses usually require a full-time commitment from a team of two or more analysts. The Offshore Patrol Cutter program maintains five full time analysts, and the Polar Icebreaker program is funding six analysts. The other major acquisition programs in FY 2017 range in support from about one-third of a work year up to a full year of funding.

CG-9283 reported that it devoted about 70 percent of a work year for each of three LCCEs completed, including time spent revising estimates after they were deemed insufficient.

A separate set of data from AIR 4.2 indicates it takes a team of two about three months to prepare the annual flying hour program budget estimate update for new acquisition aircraft.[28] This only accounts for the annual cost of repairables, consumables, and fuel usage. AIR 4.2 reported that about half this time is spent collecting data from the program office and preparing the initial estimate. The other half is spent reviewing and validating the data and estimate and getting the data through several supervisory reviews. For the Coast Guard, a similar process could probably be implemented to update annual cost analyses.

At the beginning of this research, the question was "how many more than two cost analysts in CG-9283 are needed to support the Coast Guard requirements?" Of course, finding resources to fund additional cost analysts can be very difficult. However, we determined that there are already about 20 people conducting cost analysis in CG-9283 and CG-93. Therefore, the key question the Coast Guard must now consider is "How can we better use current funding levels to improve cost-estimating performance and reduce cost-estimating gaps?" We will discuss a range of alternatives that can be considered without a significant change in required funding for cost analyses.

---

[28] K. Duke Wells, "AIR 4.2.2.3 FHP Cost Team Lead," data set, March 10, 2017.

5. Training and Manning for a Cost-Analysis Function

Traditionally, the Coast Guard has had funding for one contractor and two active-duty cost estimators. Over time, it became difficult to fill both active-duty positions because of lack of interest in the position, so the Coast Guard converted one of the active-duty positions to a government employee position, which was filled in late 2016. As a result, the Coast Guard currently uses the expertise of active-duty, civilian, and contractor cost estimators.

To gain a better understanding of the role of cost estimators, differences between levels, and the requirements needed to fulfill the role, we examined the "Certification Standards & Core Plus Development Guide."[29] We also gathered information from other sources, including the two current Coast Guard cost estimators; Department of Labor documentation for the cost-estimator position; and additional supporting documentation from the Coast Guard. This chapter documents the tasks that cost estimators perform; the knowledge, skills, and abilities (KSAs) needed to perform these tasks; and the training and experience required to obtain these KSAs.

Key Tasks of Cost Estimators

According to the Coast Guard job description for a lead cost estimator, the job is classified at the GS-15 level and typically requires training equivalent to that for an operations research analyst. A Coast Guard cost estimator has major duties:

1. developing and using methods to provide cost estimates for acquisition, deployment, and production for air, sea, and information technology systems (60 percent of time)
2. mentoring and training employees who have less experience with cost estimating (30 percent of time)
3. providing cost-estimating advice to other parts of the CG-9 organization (10 percent of time).

This specific job description was used for the cost estimator hired into a Level II position, which requires supervision of the current Level I cost estimator. Level I cost estimators would spend more time on the first task and less time on mentoring and training, as they are less likely to supervise others. Currently, this split between mentoring and training is occurring because there is one Level II civilian cost estimator, who is also the team lead for the cost estimators.

The Department of Labor's occupational network database, O*NET, has information about both cost estimators (Occupation Code 13-1051.00) and operations research analysts

---

[29] Defense Acquisition University (DAU), "Certification Standards & Core Plus Development Guide: Business Cost Estimating," web page, undated. A cost estimator might function at Levels I, II, or III, with III being the highest level. U.S. Department of Homeland Security, *Acquisition Certification Requirements for DHS Cost Estimating*, DHS Acquisition Workforce Policy No. 064-04-008, Revision 01, October 13, 2011.

(Occupation Code 15-2031.00).[30] O*NET's description of the cost-estimator position is more similar to the job description we received from the Coast Guard. Table 5.1 contains the KSAs that one needs to be a cost estimator, according to O*NET information.

Table 5.1. KSAs for Cost Estimators

Knowledge	Skills	Abilities
Mathematics	Accounting software	Inductive reasoning
Engineering and technology	Analytical or scientific software	Mathematical reasoning
English language	Database user interface and query	Number faculty
Building and construction	software	Oral comprehension
Computers and electronics	Financial analysis software	Oral expression
	Project management software	
	Mathematics	
	Critical thinking	
	Reading comprehension	
	Active listening	
	Judgment and decisionmaking	

SOURCE: National Center for O*NET Development, 2017a.

Education, Training Requirements, and Experience for Cost Estimators

The requirements to be a cost estimator at each of the three levels differ in a number of important job and training requirements. The core certification standards necessary to achieve the three levels of acquisition certification requirements for DHS cost estimating vary in acquisition training, functional training, and experience. One similarity across the three levels is the education requirement. A cost estimator must have a bachelor's degree, with at least three hours of calculus and 21 semester credit hours in operations research, economics, mathematics, chemistry, physics, or other sciences that use advanced mathematical skills (geometry, trigonometry, statistics, probability, and/or quantitative analysis). Table 5.2 summarizes the specific training requirements for different levels (note that previous cost-estimating experience is required due to DHS qualification requirements). In addition to the educational requirement, more years of practice are needed to attain higher levels.

---

[30] National Center for O*NET Development, "Summary Report for 13-1051.00—Cost Estimators," web page, O*NET OnLine, 2017a; National Center for O*NET Development, "Summary Report for 15-2031.00—Operations Research Analysts," web page, O*NET OnLine, 2017b.

Table 5.2. Training, Education, and Experience Requirements for DHS Certification

	Level I	Level II	Level III
Acquisition training	DHS AQN 101 Fundamentals of System Acquisition	DHS AQN 201A & B Intermediate System Acquisition	
Functional training	DAU BCF 102 Fundamentals of Earned Value Management DAU BCF 103 Fundamentals of Business Financial Management DAU BCF 106 Fundamentals of Cost Analysis DAU BCF 107 Applied Cost Analysis	DAU BCF 204 Intermediate Cost Analysis DAU BCF 206 Cost/Risk Analysis DAU BCF 211 Acquisition Business Management DAU BCF 215 Operating and Support Cost Analysis CLB 026 Forecasting Techniques CLB 030 Data Collection and Sources	DAU BCF 302 Advanced Concepts in Cost Analysis DAU CLB 023 Software Cost Estimating DAU CLB 029 Rates
Experience	2 years acquisition experience in cost estimating	4 years acquisition experience in cost estimating	7 years acquisition experience in cost estimating

SOURCE: DAU, undated.
NOTE: AQN = Acquisition; BCF = Business, Cost Estimating, and Financial Management; CLB = Continuous Learning Business.

Cost Analysts Will Develop Coast Guard–Specific Expertise

The professional certification levels required for cost analysis can provide a unique set of skills to support PMs and Coast Guard leadership as part of the acquisition decision process. The value added from experienced, well-trained cost analysts will be similar to the benefits of professional contract specialists and business financial managers. We have described the investment the Coast Guard needs to make to develop a professional cost organization. If a cost organization is established, it will be possible to build on the core certification requirements and develop specialized skills for ship, aviation, information technology, and operating and support cost analysis.

6. Alternatives for Fulfilling Demand for Cost-Analysis Services

In the preceding material, we have laid out the demands for Coast Guard cost-analysis services from Congress, GAO, DHS, and the Coast Guard itself. We have described the scope of activities currently being performed, whether in house or through contractor support, and we have described the cost of that contractor support both in CG-9283 and CG-93.

In this chapter, we describe three alternatives for meeting the demand for cost analysis. One alternative is to continue the current process, with no centralized control of cost analysis except when program and independent cost estimates are reconciled by CG-928. At the other end of the spectrum, the Coast Guard could develop a centralized cost-analysis organization of civil service and military officers. They would work in independent teams separately supporting program-office and independent cost estimates, but they would be supervised by a single management organization. The third alternative proposes more-centralized control of cost analysis but may include a mix of civil service, military, contractor, and interservice arrangements with NAVSEA or other acquisition commands.

Background

Describing alternatives for the Coast Guard cost-estimating capability requires an understanding of the current capability and the ability to identify one or more alternative changes to the current status. Our research has identified a broad mixture of methods for obtaining cost analysts and an equally broad mixture of methods to deliver cost-analysis products. As mentioned, the Coast Guard has two cost analysts in CG-9283 (a Coast Guard officer and one government employee), and they are responsible for preparing ICEs for major acquisition programs. For the various program offices of CG-93, there are approximately 12 to 15 FTEs of cost-estimating requirements, plus five FTEs preparing cost-related documentation for the ten current major acquisition programs in FY 2017.

CG-93 cost estimating for the program LCCEs are conducted by agreements with NAVSEA (05C) for both civil service and contractor analysts or other commercial contracts to provide qualified cost-estimating personnel. A similar relationship occurs with NAVAIR or the Air Force for aircraft-related efforts. Analytical methods and data sources to prepare LCCEs are provided in the cost-estimating baseline documents prepared independently for each program. It is not clear that data from previous LCCEs are available as analogous data for future systems.

Our interviews affirmed LCCEs were being completed within the *Major Systems Acquisition Manual* guidelines.[31] With help from a temporarily assigned DHS cost analyst to provide support

---

[31] U.S. Coast Guard, 2015.

to program teams, LCCEs are being approved through the DHS 12-step process. Acquisition programs are being approved, and systems are being delivered.

For CG-9283, the organization responsible for the ICE, the two analysts have difficulty completing ICE on time and depend on contractor support. Because this contract work is not continuous, there are significant delays between identifying the requirement for cost support and getting a contract in place to support CG-9283.

Given the list of capabilities and the gaps described in Chapter 2, there are various possible alternatives to fulfill other required activities and to improve the internal cost-analysis capability in the Coast Guard.

Alternative A

This alternative recommends no significant change: The CG-9283 branch is responsible only for ICEs. Given the fiscal situation in the Coast Guard, this alternative may be the only path forward. It would maintain the status quo and enable the CG-9283 staff to focus only on the ICEs, and it would minimize any review cycle and thus reduce any dissenting opinion because the CG-9283 analysts would not have gained greater understanding of programs by participating in program cost analyses. If CG-9283 is tasked to provide the DHS-mandated LCCE annual update, it is clear the two full-time cost analysts will require augmentation.

On the negative side, the workload fluctuations in the requirement for ICEs would make long-term manpower planning and education for the branch difficult. Management requests for modifications to the ICEs under different circumstances would be difficult for the staff to undertake. As a result, the CG-9283 staff would not be responsive to leadership requirements. Each cost analysis would be independent, and there would be little learning between the analyses. Since the staff would not be sharing information on how to perform cost analyses, each analysis would be unique and done by people and organizations that may have a stake in the outcome. This alternative would likely require contract cost-analyst support, as is the case today. That contracting mechanism has not been all that successful because different companies have different levels of understanding and expertise in this cost-analysis specialization.

Alternative B

In this alternative, all cost analysis should be conducted primarily by civil service and military personnel, managed by a single competency-aligned organization (independent of any decision on the number of Coast Guard cost estimators needed). This cost-analysis competency would build a civilian workforce, augmented by contract cost analysts only as necessary, to support CG-93 PM analyses, CG-9283 independent life-cycle cost analyses, and the recently mandated major program LCCE annual updates required by DHS. A single competency of this type would be similar to the budgeting process led by CG-82 and supervision of the business and financial management process in CG-9283.

The cost-analysis division would be divided into teams to support the complete range of CG-93 major system cost-analysis requirements. One team would be responsible for the ICEs and report to CG-9283. Cost teams should also be able to conduct the annual life-cycle updates and cost-analysis research projects to enhance professional development. Hiring, training, professional development, and promotions would be centrally controlled.

The cost competency should develop a single, standard methodology to prepare and present program and independent cost analyses. One measure to improve acceptance of cost analyses is to prepare presentations in a consistent format, which would enable decisionmakers to grasp quickly the essential elements of the cost analyses from different programs. This requirement does not impede data collection and cost analysis of program requirements but does enforce discipline preparing to explain the results of each analysis.

Alternative C

Alternative C is a compromise between Alternatives A and B, which are at opposite ends of the of the recommendation spectrum. Alternative C would retain the cost competency alignment but would use a more varied mix of hiring sources to develop the required cost products. Coast Guard cost analysis would use find an effective balance between government, interservice, and commercial contracting employees, while eventually progressing to a primarily civil service cost-analysis competency organization. The cost division would maintain centralized contracting authority to provide cost-analysis support to programs in CG-93 and CG-9283 and would ensure that all cost-analysis products meet the Coast Guard and DHS 12-step process.

Estimate of Required Billets

One of the goals of this research is to provide a recommended change in the number of cost-analysis billets in the Coast Guard. After identifying that the current level of cost-analysis work in CG-9283 and CG-93 is meeting current program and ICE timelines, the current level of about 20 FTEs appears to be approximately correct. However, if CG-9283 is to immediately take on the required annual LCCE updates, using the NAVAIR annual update analogy described in Chapter 4, we would recommend that the two additional billets already submitted in the FY 2019 budget cycle should be approved and filled as soon as possible.

A second objective of the research is to recommend any changes in sources of cost-analyst employment (i.e., civilian or contractor employees). We recommend hiring civilians to the maximum extent possible so as to create an organization fully dedicated to Coast Guard requirements.

The third objective of the study is to recommend a competency-aligned cost organization that should improve the quality of cost products and increase the confidence of senior leadership. Although it is feasible to retain two separate cost-analysis organizations, one in CG-9283 and one in CG-93, we recommend establishing a single cost division providing cost-analysis support separately to the program teams and independent cost analysis. With a single organization of 20 cost analysts, even with normal turnover and promotion, the Coast Guard will have a core capability that should be able to address the gaps in performance in Chapter 3, understanding cost methodologies, provide flexibility to meet changing requirements quickly, improve consistency in cost reporting, and create trusted agents to support PMs during cost deliberations, both with the contractors and milestone decision authorities.

7. Conclusions

The Coast Guard has recognized a requirement to improve its cost-analysis capability to support major acquisition decisions. This report responds to that requirement by describing some of the gaps in successfully completing LCCEs and proposes a range of alternatives. Our research found that there was virtually unanimous support across headquarters staff to enhance the current cost-analysis capability inside the Coast Guard.

This report provides a set of alternatives intended to foster discussion among Coast Guard leaders and develop a plan to develop a cost-analysis capability suited to their requirements. Our research confirms that the Coast Guard continues to be a unique organization with requirements that do not perfectly align with the Department of Defense or with other parts of DHS.

The research emphasizes two primary issues that will determine the structure and objectives of cost analysis within the Coast Guard:

- Should the Coast Guard centralize cost analysis within a single organization or remain as a stovepiped organization?
- Should the Coast Guard build a civil service and uniformed officer cost activity?

The three alternatives described here attempt to identify strengths and weakness of various alternative solutions.

As with the Department of Defense, DHS and Coast Guard leadership will continue to face affordability and life-cycle cost issues (during the FY 2017 Continuing Resolution debates, the commandant of the Coast Guard, ADM Paul Zukunft, stated that he was worried about operations and maintenance).[32]

To comply with the directions coming from DHS and, more important, from Coast Guard leadership, the Coast Guard needs a more robust cost-estimating capability that can fully understand the models and data used to predict cost. The Coast Guard also needs an ability to respond to "what if" questions from higher-level management. Knowledge of the models and data being used are intrinsic to that ability. The Coast Guard may still be able to contract out portions of the work, but it needs clear visibility into estimation methods. Based on the work currently being contracted out and the overall demand, our estimate is that the Coast Guard can support and benefit from a competency-based cost-analysis division of about 22 people.

---

[32] Sydney J. Freedberg, Jr., "Coast Guard Dodges Big Trump Budget Bullet; But Coasties Fix Roofs," *Breaking Defense*, April 12, 2017.

Bibliography

Center for Naval Analyses, "Evaluation of Systems Command Consolidation Options, Phase 2," July 2015.

Crumpacker, Jim H., "DHS Management Response to Recommendations Contained in GAO-17-218," Department of Homeland Security, February 16, 2017.

DAU—*See* Defense Acquisition University.

Defense Acquisition University, "Certification Standards & Core Plus Development Guide: Business Cost Estimating," web page, undated. As of May 17, 2017: http://icatalog.dau.mil/onlinecatalog/CareerLvl.aspx?lvl=1&cfld=17

Freedberg, Sydney J., Jr., "Coast Guard Dodges Big Trump Budget Bullet; But Coasties Fix Roofs," *Breaking Defense*, April 12, 2017.

Fulghum, Chip, "Annual Cost Estimates," Department of Homeland Security, January 11, 2016.

———, "Mastering Acquisition Oversight List," Department of Homeland Security, February 2, 2017.

GAO—*See* U.S. Government Accountability Office.

National Center for O*NET Development, "Summary Report for 13-1051.00—Cost Estimators," web page, O*NET OnLine, 2017a. As of May 22, 2017: https://www.onetonline.org/link/summary/13-1051.00

———, "Summary Report for 15-2031.00—Operations Research Analysts," web page, O*NET OnLine, 2017b. As of May 22, 2017: https://www.onetonline.org/link/summary/15-2031.00

Secretary of the Navy, Instruction 5223.2A, "Department of the Navy Cost Analysis," Washington, D.C.: Department of the Navy, December 3, 2012a.

———, Instruction 5420.196A, "Establishment and Review of Department of the Navy Independent Cost Estimates for Acquisition Category's IC and IA Programs," Washington, D.C.: Department of the Navy, December 3, 2012b.

———, Instruction 7000.29, "Naval Visibility and Management of Operating and Support Costs Program Data Collection," Washington, D.C.: Department of the Navy, November 15, 2016.

Streett, Bryant, Jennifer Jacobs, Phillip Keller, Sarah Menon, Hans Petry, Peter Vanden Bosch, Steven Weiss, Mark Hanson, and Richard Kohout, *Analysis of Alternatives (AoA)*

Methodologies: Considerations for DHS Acquisition Analysis, Falls Church, Va.: Homeland Security Studies and Analysis Institute, January 22, 2014.

U.S. Coast Guard, *Coast Guard Acquisition Management Roles and Responsibilities*, Commandant Instruction 5000.12, July 6, 2012.

———, *Reimbursable Standard Rates*, Commandant Instruction 7310.1Q, October 16, 2015.

———, *Acquisition Directorate Strategic Plan: Blueprint for Sustained Excellence*, version 6.1, Summer 2016.

U.S. Coast Guard, Acquisition Directorate, *Non-Major Acquisition Process (NMAP) Manual*, Commandant Instruction M5000.11B, December 2012.

———, *Major Systems Acquisition Manual (MSAM)*, Commandant Instruction M5000.10D, May 29, 2015.

U.S. Department of Defense, "Operation of the Defense Acquisition System," Department of Defense Instruction 5000.02, January 7, 2012, revised February 2, 2017.

U.S. Department of Homeland Security, *Acquisition Certification Requirements for DHS Cost Estimating*, DHS Acquisition Workforce Policy No. 064-04-008, Revision 01, October 13, 2011.

———, "Acquisition Management Directive," Directive Number: 102-01, Revision Number 3, July 28, 2015.

———, *United States Coast Guard, Fiscal Year 2017: Congressional Justification*, 2016.

———, "Acquisition Management Instruction," DHS Instruction 102-01-001, Revision 1, March 19, 2016.

U.S. Government Accountability Office, *GAO Cost Estimating and Assessment Guide*, Washington, D.C., GAO-09-3SP, March 2009.

———, *Homeland Security Acquisitions: DHS Should Better Define Oversight Roles and Improve Program Reporting to Congress*, GAO-15-292, March 2015. As of May 11, 2017: https://www.gao.gov/assets/670/668975.pdf

U.S. House of Representatives, DHS Acquisition Documentation Integrity Act of 2017, 115th Cong., 1st sess., H.R. 347, January 31, 2017a.

———, DHS Acquisition Authorities Act of 2017, 115th Cong., 1st sess., H.R. 1252, March 21, 2017b.

———, Department of Homeland Security Acquisition Innovation Act, 115th Cong., 1st sess., H.R. 1365, March 27, 2017c.

Wells, K. Duke, "AIR 4.2.2.3 FHP Cost Team Lead," data set, March 10, 2017.